The System That Cannot Be Told the Truth - The Blindness Protocol.

Published by LGIS, LLC
St. Louis, Missouri

ISBN: 979-8-9971013-3-6

Library of Congress Control Number: 2026923219

Printed in the United States of America.

For my children, who watched me rebuild myself.

For my parents, who taught me what strength looks like.

And for the professor who rewired the way I write and set me on the path to this book.

Table of Contents

Author's Preface

Blindness does not emerge from missing information. Blindness emerges when institutional identity makes certain truths incompatible with survival. Once identity becomes defensive, accuracy becomes impossible. Contradiction becomes threat. Correction becomes forbidden. Truth becomes structurally unabsorbable.

Blindness is not failure. Blindness is the architecture.

This book exposes that architecture.

Prologue — The Rules of Unintended Consequences

Afghanistan → CIA → Proxy Logic → Corporate Blindness

Every system believes it understands the consequences of its actions.
Every system is wrong.

Afghanistan is the place where this truth became impossible to ignore.
Not because the war was unique, but because it exposed a pattern that had been repeating for decades:
powerful institutions creating outcomes they never intended.
mechanisms they never examined.
architectures they never understood.

The CIA did not enter Afghanistan to build a future.
It entered to solve a problem.

The problem was Soviet expansion.
The solution was proxy warfare.
The mechanism was simple:

- find actors whose interests temporarily align with yours.
- arm them.
- train them.
- fund them.
- let them absorb the risk you cannot afford to carry yourself.

Proxy logic is elegant.
Proxy logic is efficient.
Proxy logic is blind.

Because proxy logic always assumes the proxy will remain a proxy.
It assumes alignment will remain alignment.
It assumes control will remain control.
It assumes the system can shape outcomes.
It assumes the system will not absorb consequences.

Afghanistan proved otherwise.

The CIA built a network it believed it controlled.
It built an ecosystem it believed it understood.
It built a future it believed it could manage.

It built unintended consequences.

The actors the CIA empowered did not remain proxies.
They became independent systems with their own identities, their own ambitions, their own trajectories.
The CIA created an architecture to solve one problem.
That architecture generated another.

This is the rule of unintended consequences.
The system that solves the problem becomes the system that creates the next one.

And this rule does not belong to intelligence agencies alone.

Corporations follow it with the same precision.

The CEO who believes their enterprise is “different” from every case study they read in business school is reenacting the same blindness that guided proxy warfare.

The MBA who believes their strategy is immune to unintended consequences is reenacting the same operational arrogance that shaped Afghanistan.

The board that believes its governance structure can absorb any shock is reenacting the same narrative confidence that collapsed under geopolitical reality.

Corporate systems outsource risk the same way intelligence agencies outsource conflict.

They build proxies:

- vendors
- contractors
- subsidiaries
- offshore teams
- consultants
- "innovation labs"
- "skunkworks"
- "autonomous units"

Each proxy is treated as controllable.
Each proxy is treated as aligned.
Each proxy is treated as an extension of the system's will.

Until it isn't.

The same physics apply:

- alignment becomes divergence
- divergence becomes independence
- independence becomes consequence
- consequence becomes collapse

The CIA did not intend to create the conditions that destabilized the region.
Corporations do not intend to create the conditions that destabilize their enterprises.

But systems do not collapse because they intend to.
Systems collapse because they cannot see their own

architecture.
Systems collapse because they cannot see its consequences.

This book is about that blindness.

Not ideological blindness.
Not moral blindness.
Not cultural blindness.

Structural blindness.

The blindness that emerges when systems protect identity at the expense of accuracy.
The blindness that emerges when institutions outsource risk without understanding what they are outsourcing.
The blindness that emerges when leaders believe their situation is unique, their strategy is exceptional, their proxies are controllable, their consequences are predictable.

Afghanistan is not a metaphor.
It is a case study in how systems create futures they cannot survive.

The CIA is not an outlier.
It is an example of how institutions generate blindness through the very mechanisms they use to maintain control.

Corporate governance is not separate.
It is the civilian expression of the same architecture.

This book is not about Afghanistan.
It is not about the CIA.
It is not about corporations.

It is about the **system that produces unintended consequences** —
and the blindness that prevents institutions from seeing them until they become unavoidable

SECTION I
Diagnostic Architecture

Chapter One — Identity Fracture

How Systems Break Their Own Definition Before They Break Their Own Future
Afghanistan → CIA → Corporate Governance

Identity fracture is the first step toward blindness.
Systems do not lie to themselves.
Systems define themselves in ways that cannot survive the conditions they operate in.
Afghanistan is where this fracture became visible.

The CIA entered the region with a clear identity:
a precision instrument designed to shape geopolitical outcomes without direct exposure.
Its operational identity was built on control.
Its operational identity was built on alignment.
Its operational identity was built on plausible deniability.
Its institutional identity was built on the belief that it could manage complexity through proxies.

This identity could not survive Afghanistan.
Afghanistan made that identity impossible

Proxy warfare requires a stable definition of "us" and "them."
But Afghanistan did not offer that stability.
It offered tribes, factions, alliances that shifted weekly, loyalties that were transactional, and actors whose motivations were older than the United States itself.

The CIA's identity — "we control the proxy" — fractured the moment the proxy became an independent system.

The fracture was not ideological.
It was architectural.

The CIA believed it was shaping the future.
It was shaping actors who would later define their own futures.
Futures the CIA could not control.
Futures the CIA could not predict.
Futures the CIA could not absorb.

This is identity fracture:
the moment a system's definition becomes incompatible with its environment.

The same physics apply to corporations.

A CEO enters a market believing their enterprise is unique.
They believe their strategy is exceptional.
They believe their culture is distinct.
They believe their governance structure is resilient.

This identity fractures the moment the enterprise meets conditions it cannot control.
Conditions that do not care about its narrative.

The MBA case-study mindset — "we are different" — is the corporate version of proxy warfare.
It is the belief that the system can shape outcomes without absorbing consequences.
It is the belief that the enterprise can outsource risk to vendors, contractors, offshore teams, consultants, and innovation labs without losing control.

This identity fractures the moment those proxies become independent systems.

A vendor becomes indispensable.
A contractor becomes irreplaceable.
A subsidiary becomes autonomous.
A consultant becomes the de facto strategist.
An offshore team becomes the operational backbone.

The enterprise's identity — "we control the proxy" — fractures the moment the proxy becomes the system.

Identity fracture is not failure.
Identity fracture is the beginning.
Unintended consequences begin here.

The CIA did not intend to create actors who would later destabilize the region.
Corporations do not intend to create dependencies that later destabilize their governance.

But systems do not fracture because they intend to.
Systems fracture because their identity cannot absorb the conditions they operate in.

Identity fracture is the moment the system generates outcomes it cannot reconcile.
Outcomes that contradict its definition..

In Afghanistan, the contradiction was geopolitical.
In corporations, the contradiction is operational.

In both cases, the fracture emerges from the same mechanism:

the system defines itself by what it wants to be, not by what the environment requires it to be.

Identity fracture is the first step toward blindness because it forces the system to choose between revising its definition or protecting it.

The CIA protected its definition.
Corporations protect theirs.

Revision feels destabilizing.
Protection feels coherent.

Coherence becomes blindness.

Identity fracture is not the collapse of the system.
It is the collapse of the system's ability to see itself.

This is where the blindness protocol begins.
Not with deception.
Not with arrogance.
With identity.

The system fractures long before it fails.
It fractures the moment it insists on being something the environment cannot sustain.

Afghanistan revealed this.
Corporate governance reenacts it.
Proxy logic amplifies it.
Unintended consequences expose it.

Identity fracture is the first architecture of blindness.
It is the moment the system begins protecting the definition that will later destroy it.

Chapter Two — Distortion Field

How Systems Misinterpret Their Own Signals Until Reality Breaks Through
Proxy Warfare → Corporate KPIs → Operational Misperception

Distortion doesn't begin when a system receives bad information.
Distortion begins when a system **ignores information it already has**.

The CIA did not misread Afghanistan because Afghanistan was opaque.
It misread Afghanistan because it walked in with a pre-distorted lens.
A lens shaped by decades of proxy warfare in Central America.

Guatemala.
Cuba.
Dominican Republic.
Nicaragua.
El Salvador.
Honduras.
Chile.

Every one of these operations produced the same pattern.
proxies drift
proxies radicalize
proxies pursue their own agendas
proxies generate blowback
blowback becomes geopolitical consequence

The CIA had already lived through this.
It had already documented it.
It had already buried officers because of it.
It had already destabilized governments because of it.

The pattern was not subtle.
The pattern was not ambiguous.
The pattern was not theoretical.
The pattern was historical.
The pattern was fact.

Yet when Afghanistan emerged, the CIA treated it as a clean slate — a "different category" of conflict, a "unique opportunity," a "safe proxy war" with "no long-term cost."

This is distortion.
The system ignores signals from its own past.
Signals that contradict the identity it wants to protect.

The CIA did not misinterpret Afghanistan.
It misinterpreted itself.

It believed:

- "This proxy will stay aligned."
- "This proxy will dissolve after victory."
- "This proxy will not pursue independent ambitions."
- "This proxy will not generate blowback."

These beliefs were not based on evidence.
They were based on **institutional identity** — the belief that the CIA could control outcomes because it needed to believe it could.

Distortion is not misreading the environment.
Distortion is misreading your own history.
Distortion is misreading what you already lived.

The same physics apply to corporations.

Corporate KPIs are not misinterpreted because they are unclear.
They are misinterpreted because leaders ignore previous

cycles.
Cycles where KPIs produced catastrophic misalignment.

Every enterprise has its own "Banana Republics":

- the vendor that drifted
- the contractor that became indispensable
- the offshore team that became the operational backbone
- the consultant that became the de facto strategist
- the innovation lab that became a rogue unit

Every enterprise has lived through proxy drift.
Every enterprise has seen unintended consequences.
Every enterprise has experienced blowback.

Yet every new initiative is treated as a clean slate:

- "This vendor is different."
- "This contractor is aligned."
- "This KPI reflects reality."
- "This dashboard is objective."
- "This strategy is unique."

This is distortion:
the enterprise ignores its own history because the history contradicts the identity it wants to protect.

Just like the CIA.

Distortion is not noise.
Distortion is architecture.

It emerges when:

- the system protects identity over accuracy
- the system treats past failures as irrelevant
- the system treats past blowback as anomalies
- the system treats past drift as exceptions

- the system treats past consequences as unrelated

Afghanistan was not a surprise.
It was a repetition.

Corporate collapse is not a surprise.
It is a repetition.

Distortion is the moment the system becomes confident in conclusions that contradict its own history.

This is the second architecture of blindness.
Identity fracture breaks definition.
Distortion breaks memory.

Once memory breaks, the system begins generating decisions based on signals it *wants* to believe — not signals it has already learned to fear.

Afghanistan showed this.
Central America proved it.
Corporate governance reenacts it.
KPIs institutionalize it.

Chapter Three — Anesthesia Layer

How Systems Numb Contradiction to Protect Identity
Afghanistan → CIA → Corporate Governance

Anesthesia is not silence.
Anesthesia is the moment a system stops reacting.
Signals that should force it to change.

Afghanistan made this visible long before the first proxy was armed.

The CIA had already lived through the consequences of proxy warfare in Central America.
It had already seen how "temporary allies" become permanent actors.
It had already seen how "controlled operations" become uncontrollable ecosystems.
It had already seen how "short-term interventions" become long-term instability.

The contradictions were not subtle.
They were documented.
They were archived.
They were taught internally.
They became institutional memory.

Yet when Afghanistan emerged, the CIA behaved as if none of that history existed.

This is anesthesia.
The system numbs contradictions that threaten its identity.

The contradiction was simple:

- Proxy warfare produces blowback.
- Proxy warfare in Afghanistan would produce blowback.

- The CIA did not want to believe this.

So it didn't.

Not because the evidence was missing.
Because the evidence was incompatible with the identity the CIA needed to protect:

"We can control this."

Anesthesia is not denial.
Anesthesia is operational numbness.
The system continues acting.
Even when signals contradict the action.

The CIA numbed:

- the warnings from analysts
- the lessons from Central America
- the documented blowback patterns
- the internal dissent
- the geopolitical risk models
- the historical precedent

Not because it lacked intelligence.
Because it lacked permission.
Permission to revise identity.

The same anesthesia exists inside corporations.

Corporate governance is filled with contradictions that should force revision:

- KPIs that contradict market reality
- vendor dependencies that contradict autonomy
- consultant influence that contradict leadership
- offshore reliance that contradict resilience
- innovation labs that contradict control
- "unique strategy" narratives that contradict history

Every enterprise has lived through these contradictions.
Every enterprise has seen the blowback.
Every enterprise has experienced drift.

Yet every enterprise behaves as if each new initiative is immune.

This is anesthesia:
the enterprise numbs the contradictions that threaten the identity it wants to protect.

A CEO sees a KPI spike that contradicts customer feedback.
And feels nothing.
A board sees a vendor dependency that contradicts resilience.
And feels nothing.
A strategy team sees a market shift that contradicts the roadmap.
And feels nothing.
An MBA sees a case-study pattern repeating inside their own enterprise.
And feels nothing.

Not because the signals are unclear.
Because the signals are incompatible with the identity the enterprise needs to preserve:

"We are different."

Anesthesia is not ignorance.
Anesthesia is institutional self-protection.
Protection that replaces adaptation.

It emerges when:

- the system cannot absorb contradiction
- contradiction threatens identity
- identity protects coherence
- coherence protects operation

- operation protects survival

The system numbs the contradiction.
Instead of revising identity.

Afghanistan showed this.
Corporate governance reenacts it.
Proxy logic amplifies it.
Unintended consequences expose it.

Anesthesia is the third architecture of blindness.

Identity fracture breaks definition.
Distortion breaks memory.
Anesthesia breaks sensation.

Once sensation breaks, the system stops reacting to the very signals that would have saved it.

The CIA did not fail to see Afghanistan.
It failed to *feel* Afghanistan.

Corporations do not fail to see drift.
They fail to *feel* drift.

Anesthesia is the moment the system becomes comfortable.
Comfortable with contradictions that should terrify it..

It is the moment blindness becomes emotional.
It is the moment unintended consequences become inevitable.
It is the moment the system begins accelerating toward outcomes it cannot survive.

Anesthesia is not the collapse of the system.
It is the collapse of the system's ability to respond.

This is where the blindness protocol deepens.
Not with deception.

Not with distortion.
With numbness.

The system stops feeling the consequences of its own architecture — and begins generating futures it cannot absorb.

Chapter Four — Acceleration

How Systems Speed Up When They Should Slow Down
Afghanistan → CIA → Corporate Governance

Acceleration is not momentum.
Acceleration is panic.
Panic disguised as strategy.

It is the moment a system increases intensity.
The same actions producing unintended consequences.
Not because acceleration is rational.
Because slowing down would force confrontation.
Confronting contradictions the system has anesthetized.

Afghanistan made this unavoidable.

By the early 1980s, the CIA had already seen the blowback patterns from Central America.
It had already seen how proxies drift.
It had already seen how proxies radicalize.
It had already seen how proxies pursue their own agendas.
It had already seen how proxies become independent systems.

These were not hypotheticals.
They were historical.
They were facts.

Yet instead of slowing down, the CIA accelerated.

More weapons.
More funding.
More training.
More autonomy.
More operational latitude.
More reliance on actors whose incentives were never aligned with American interests.

Acceleration was not strategic.
Acceleration was anesthetic.
Anesthesia disguised as motion.

It allowed the CIA to avoid confronting the contradiction:

"We are empowering actors we cannot control."

Slowing down would have forced revision.
Revision of identity.
Acceleration protected identity.

Acceleration is the system's attempt to outrun the consequences of its own architecture.

The same physics apply to corporations.

When KPIs begin contradicting market reality, enterprises accelerate:

- more hiring
- more spending
- more initiatives
- more vendors
- more consultants
- more offshore expansion
- more "innovation labs"
- more dashboards
- more strategy decks

Acceleration becomes the default response.
The default response to contradiction.

A CEO sees a warning signal — and accelerates.
A board sees a dependency — and accelerates.
A strategy team sees a market shift — and accelerates.
An MBA sees a case-study pattern repeating — and accelerates.

Acceleration is not confidence.
Acceleration is fear.
It is the moment the enterprise increases intensity.
The same actions destabilizing it

Just like Afghanistan.

Acceleration emerges when:

- identity fracture breaks definition
- distortion breaks memory
- anesthesia breaks sensation

Once sensation breaks, the system cannot feel.
It cannot feel the contradiction.
Once memory breaks, the system cannot recall.
It cannot recall the precedent.
Once definition breaks, the system cannot revise.
It cannot revise identity.

Acceleration becomes inevitable.

The CIA accelerated proxy warfare because slowing down would have forced it to confront the blowback it already knew was coming.
Corporations accelerate initiatives because slowing down would force them to confront the drift they already know is happening.

Acceleration is the fourth architecture of blindness.

Identity fracture breaks definition.
Distortion breaks memory.
Anesthesia breaks sensation.
Acceleration breaks control.

Once control breaks, the system begins generating futures it cannot manage.

Afghanistan showed this.
Corporate governance reenacts it.
Proxy logic amplifies it.
Unintended consequences expose it.

Acceleration is not the collapse of the system.
Acceleration is the collapse of the system's ability to regulate itself.

It is the moment the system speeds toward outcomes it cannot survive — because slowing down would require becoming something it cannot yet admit it needs to be.

Acceleration is not momentum.
Acceleration is blindness.
Blindness in motion.

Chapter Five — Return Pressure

How Consequences Come Back Through the Same Channels That Created Them
Afghanistan → CIA → Corporate Governance

Return pressure is not retaliation.
Return pressure is the moment a system absorbs consequences.
Consequences traveling through the same pathways it used to avoid them.

Afghanistan is the clearest example of this in modern history.

The CIA believed proxy warfare insulated it from risk.
It believed proxies absorbed consequences.
It believed proxies carried the operational burden.
It believed proxies created distance between action and accountability.

Proxy logic assumes consequences travel outward.
But consequences travel inward.

The actors the CIA empowered did not remain proxies.
They became independent systems.
Systems with their own identities.
Systems with their own incentives.
Systems with their own trajectories.

The weapons the CIA supplied returned as threats.
The training the CIA provided returned as capability.
The autonomy the CIA granted returned as independence.
The alliances the CIA formed returned as geopolitical constraints.

Return pressure is not blowback.
Blowback is the event.
Return pressure is architecture.

The CIA built channels to project influence.
Those channels became the pathways through which consequences returned.

This is the rule of unintended consequences:
the system must eventually absorb the outcomes it outsourced.

The same physics apply to corporations.

Corporate governance treats proxies — vendors, contractors, offshore teams, consultants, subsidiaries — as buffers.
They are supposed to absorb risk.
They are supposed to carry operational load.
They are supposed to create distance between decision and consequence.

But proxies do not absorb consequences.
They redirect them.

A vendor dependency becomes a supply-chain failure.
A contractor misalignment becomes a product defect.
An offshore team outage becomes a global operational halt.
A consultant's misdiagnosis becomes a strategic collapse.
A subsidiary's autonomy becomes a governance crisis.

The enterprise built channels to outsource risk.
Those channels become pathways.
Pathways through which risk returns.

Return pressure is not failure.
Return pressure is physics.
Physics that cannot be avoided.

It emerges when:

- the system outsources risk
- the proxy internalizes the risk

- the proxy transforms the risk
- the transformed risk returns through the same channel
- the system is forced to absorb what it created

Afghanistan made this unavoidable.
Corporate governance reenacts it.
Proxy logic amplifies it.
Unintended consequences expose it.

Return pressure is the fifth architecture of blindness.

Identity fracture breaks definition.
Distortion breaks memory.
Anesthesia breaks sensation.
Acceleration breaks control.
Return pressure breaks insulation.

Once insulation breaks, the system is forced to confront consequences.
Consequences it believed it had avoided.

The CIA did not intend to empower actors who would later destabilize the region.
Corporations do not intend to empower proxies who later destabilize their enterprise.

But systems do not absorb consequences because they intend to.
Systems absorb consequences because consequences follow architecture.

Return pressure is the moment the system realizes the truth.
The channels built to project influence.
Are the channels through which influence returns.

It is the moment the system confronts the future it created.
It is the moment unintended consequences become

unavoidable.
It is the moment blindness becomes visible.

Return pressure is not collapse.
Return pressure is the beginning.
The beginning of collapse.

It is the moment the system can no longer pretend that consequences belong to someone else.

Chapter Six — Immunity

How Systems Become Resistant to the Information That Could Save Them
Afghanistan → CIA → Corporate Governance

Immunity is not ignorance.
Immunity is the moment a system becomes structurally incapable.
Incapable of integrating information that contradicts its identity..

Afghanistan made this visible long before the first unintended consequence surfaced.

By the mid-1980s, the CIA had accumulated decades of operational intelligence from Central America:

- proxies drift
- proxies radicalize
- proxies pursue their own agendas
- proxies generate blowback
- blowback becomes geopolitical consequence

This was not theory.
This was institutional memory.

Analysts warned that Afghanistan was following the same pattern.
Field officers reported proxy drift.
Regional experts documented ideological divergence.
Internal memos flagged long-term risk.
Historical precedent pointed to blowback.
Blowback that was inevitable.

The CIA had all the information it needed.

But it could not absorb it.

Not because the information was unclear.
Because the information was incompatible with the identity the CIA needed to protect:

"We can control this."

Immunity is not the absence of intelligence.
Immunity is the refusal of intelligence.
Intelligence the system cannot absorb.

It emerges when:

- identity fracture breaks definition
- distortion breaks memory
- anesthesia breaks sensation
- acceleration breaks control
- return pressure breaks insulation

Once insulation breaks, the system is exposed to consequences.
But it still cannot revise identity.

This is immunity:
the system becomes resistant to the very information that could prevent collapse.

The CIA was not blind to Afghanistan.
It was immune.
Immune to Afghanistan.

It could not integrate:

- historical precedent
- internal warnings
- proxy drift
- ideological divergence
- operational risk
- long-term consequence

Integrating any of these would require revision.
Revision of the identity that justified the operation.

The same immunity exists inside corporations.
Corporations reenact immunity with precision

Corporate governance is filled with information that contradicts the enterprise's identity:

- KPIs that contradict customer reality
- vendor dependencies that contradict autonomy
- consultant influence that contradict leadership
- offshore reliance that contradict resilience
- innovation labs that contradict control
- market signals that contradict strategy

Executives see these contradictions.
Boards see them.
Analysts see them.
Operators see them.

But the enterprise cannot absorb them.

Not because the information is unclear.
Because the information is incompatible.
Incompatible with the identity the enterprise needs to protect:
"We are different."

Immunity is not a failure of intelligence.
Immunity is a failure of permission.
Permission the system refuses to grant itself.

The system does not allow itself to integrate information that threatens identity — even when that information is the only thing that could prevent collapse.

This is why unintended consequences feel inevitable.
They are not inevitable.
They are unabsorbed.

Afghanistan showed this.
Corporate governance reenacts it.
Proxy logic amplifies it.
Unintended consequences expose it.

Immunity is the sixth architecture of blindness.

Identity fracture breaks definition.
Distortion breaks memory.
Anesthesia breaks sensation.
Acceleration breaks control.
Return pressure breaks insulation.
Immunity breaks adaptation.

Once adaptation breaks, the system becomes incapable of changing — even when change is the only path to survival.

Immunity is not collapse.
Immunity is the moment collapse begins.
Collapse becomes irreversible.

It is the moment the system cannot revise identity.
It is the moment the system cannot integrate contradiction.
It is the moment the system cannot absorb consequence.
It is the moment the system cannot escape the architecture it built.

Immunity is the final stage of blindness.
It is the moment the system becomes resistant to the truth — and begins accelerating toward outcomes it cannot survive.

Chapter Seven — Collapse

The Moment the System Encounters the Future It Created
Afghanistan → CIA → Corporate Governance

Collapse is not the moment a system fails.
Collapse is the moment a system cannot maintain distance.
Distance between its identity and its reality.

Afghanistan is the clearest modern example of this.

By 1979, the CIA already possessed the proxy-war physics it had refined across Cuba, the Dominican Republic, Chile, Laos, and Angola.
It carried that physics directly into Afghanistan when the Soviet invasion triggered its engagement.
By the late 1980s, every architecture of blindness was already in place.

Identity fracture: The CIA defined itself as a force that could control proxies.
Distortion: It ignored its own history in Central America.
Anesthesia: It numbed contradictions that should have forced revision.
Acceleration: It intensified the very actions producing future instability.
Return pressure: Consequences began flowing back through the same channels that created them.
Immunity: The institution became resistant to the information that could have saved it.

Collapse was not a surprise.
Collapse was the only outcome.
Collapse was inevitable.

The actors the CIA empowered did not dissolve.
Not after the Soviet withdrawal.
They consolidated power.

They built networks.
They built ideology.
They built infrastructure.
They built futures.

The CIA believed it was shaping the region.
It was shaping the forces that would later reshape global security.

Collapse is not the moment the system loses control.
Collapse is the moment the system realizes the truth.
It never had control.

The same physics apply to corporations.

Corporate governance follows the identical sequence:

- identity fracture ("we are different")
- distortion (ignoring previous cycles of drift)
- anesthesia (numbing contradictions in KPIs, vendors, strategy)
- acceleration (more initiatives, more spending, more dashboards)
- return pressure (risk returning through outsourced channels)
- immunity (resistance to corrective information)

Collapse is not the moment the enterprise fails.
Collapse is the moment the enterprise becomes unable to maintain the narrative that kept it insulated from reality.

A vendor outage becomes a global operational halt.
A KPI illusion becomes a strategic misfire.
A consultant's misdiagnosis becomes a governance crisis.
An offshore dependency becomes a systemic vulnerability.
A "unique strategy" becomes a repetition of every case study the CEO insisted did not apply.

Collapse is not catastrophic.
Collapse is corrective.
Correction disguised as failure.

It is the moment the system is forced to confront the architecture it built:

- the proxies it empowered
- the incentives it ignored
- the contradictions it numbed
- the acceleration it justified
- the consequences it outsourced
- the information it refused to absorb

Collapse is not the destruction of the system.
Collapse is the destruction of identity.
The system's identity.

Afghanistan proved this.
Corporate governance reenacts it.
Proxy logic guarantees it.
Unintended consequences expose it.

Collapse is the moment the system encounters the future it created.
And realizes it cannot survive as the thing it used to be.

Collapse is not the end.
Collapse is the end of blindness.

It is the moment the system becomes visible to itself.
It is the moment the system can no longer pretend.
It is the moment the system must either revise identity or be destroyed by it.

Collapse is not failure.
Collapse is revelation.
Collapse reveals the architecture.
Revelation does not dismantle it.

After collapse, the system does not transform.
After collapse, the system stabilizes itself.
It protects identity.
It reenacts blindness

The persistence arc begins here in the architecture that keeps collapse alive.

SECTION II
Persistence Architecture

Chapter One — Coherence

How Systems Protect Identity Even After Collapse Begins
Afghanistan → CIA → Corporate Governance

Coherence is not stability.
Coherence is the system's last attempt to preserve identity.
Preserve identity after collapse has already started.

It is the moment the system insists its definition is still correct.
Even as every signal proves otherwise.
Every consequence.
Every piece of evidence.

Afghanistan made this visible in real time.

By the late 1980s, collapse was already underway:

- proxies had drifted
- ideology had hardened
- networks had consolidated
- unintended consequences had surfaced
- return pressure was flowing back
- immunity had blocked adaptation

The CIA was not confused.
It was coherent.
Coherence replaced confusion

Coherence is the system's refusal to revise identity.
Even when reality demands revision.

The CIA maintained the narrative:

"We shaped the region."
"We controlled the proxies."

"We prevented Soviet expansion."
"We stabilized the future."

None of these statements were true.
All of them were coherent.

Coherence is not accuracy.
Coherence is consistency.
Consistency without truth.

It is the moment the system protects the story that justifies its existence — even when that story no longer matches the world.

The CIA did not revise its identity.
It reinforced identity.
Reinforced the narrative that protected it.

It reframed blowback as anomaly.
It reframed proxy drift as local politics.
It reframed unintended consequences as unforeseeable.
It reframed collapse as external failure.

This is coherence.
The system maintains narrative alignment.
Even when operational alignment has already failed.

The same physics apply to corporations.

Corporate governance clings to coherence long after collapse begins:

- KPIs contradict reality → "The model is correct."
- vendor dependency becomes risk → "The partnership is strategic."
- consultant misdiagnosis becomes drift → "The framework is sound."
- offshore fragility becomes vulnerability → "The team is reliable."

- market signals contradict strategy → “The roadmap is right.”

Executives do not revise identity.
Executives reinforce identity.
Reinforcement replaces revision.

Boards do not revise governance.
They defend it.

Strategy teams do not revise assumptions.
They rationalize them.

Coherence is not leadership.
Coherence is self-protection.
Protection disguised as leadership.

It emerges when:

- collapse has begun
- consequences are visible
- drift is undeniable
- identity is incompatible with reality
- but revising identity feels existentially dangerous

So the system chooses coherence over accuracy.

Just like Afghanistan.

Coherence is the first architecture of persistence — the mechanism that allows blindness to survive collapse.

It is the moment the system becomes more committed to its narrative than to its survival.

Coherence is not the collapse of the system.
Coherence is the collapse of the system's ability to tell the truth.
Truth becomes impossible.

It is the moment the system begins rewriting reality to preserve identity.
It is the moment unintended consequences become irreversible.
It is the moment the system becomes trapped inside the story it created.

Coherence is not stability.
Coherence is inertia.
Inertia disguised as stability.

It is the moment the system continues being what it used to be — even when the environment no longer allows it.

Afghanistan showed this.
Corporate governance reenacts it.
Proxy logic guarantees it.
Unintended consequences expose it.

Coherence is the architecture that keeps blindness alive after collapse begins.

Chapter Two — Narrative

How Systems Rewrite Reality to Preserve Identity
Afghanistan → CIA → Corporate Governance

Narrative is not storytelling.
Narrative is the system's final defense.
Final defense against collapse.

It is the mechanism through which institutions rewrite reality.
Rewrite reality so identity can remain intact.
Even when reality has already invalidated it.

Afghanistan made this unavoidable.
Unavoidable in every architecture.

By the time the Soviet withdrawal was complete, the CIA's operational identity had already failed:

- **proxies were autonomous**
- **ideology had hardened**
- **unintended consequences were visible**
- **blowback was inevitable**
- **collapse had begun**

But the CIA did not revise its identity.
It revised its narrative.
Narrative replaced revision.

Narrative is the system's attempt to make collapse coherent.
Collapse made coherent through story.

The CIA reframed the operation:

"We defeated the Soviets."
"We liberated Afghanistan."
"We empowered freedom fighters."

"We stabilized the region."
"We prevented global expansion."

None of these statements were accurate.
All of them were coherent.

Narrative is not truth.
Narrative is alignment.
Coherence replaced accuracy.

It is the moment the institution rewrites events.
Events that continue to support identity.
Identity it refuses to revise.

The CIA did not describe Afghanistan.
It described a version of Afghanistan.
A version that allowed the institution to remain what it believed itself to be

This is narrative.
The system rewrites reality to preserve identity.

The same physics apply to corporations.

Corporate governance rewrites reality with the same precision.
KPIs contradict market reality → "The model is correct."
vendor dependency becomes risk → "The partnership is strategic."
consultant misdiagnosis becomes drift → "The framework is sound."
offshore fragility becomes vulnerability → "The team is reliable."
market shifts contradict strategy → "The roadmap is right."

Executives do not revise identity.
Executives revise narrative.
Narrative replaces identity revision.

Boards do not revise governance.
They revise narrative.

Strategy teams do not revise assumptions.
They revise narrative.

Narrative is not deception.
Narrative is self-preservation.
Preservation disguised as truth.

It emerges when:

- collapse has begun
- coherence has failed
- consequences are visible
- identity is incompatible with reality
- but revising identity feels existentially dangerous

So the system rewrites reality instead.
Reality rewritten to protect identity.

Just like Afghanistan.

Narrative is the second architecture of persistence — the mechanism that allows blindness to survive collapse.

It is the moment the system becomes more committed to its story than to its survival.

Narrative is not the collapse of the system.
Narrative is the collapse of the system's ability to describe reality.
Reality becomes indescribable.

It is the moment the institution begins generating explanations that protect identity rather than illuminate truth.
It is the moment unintended consequences become irreversible.
It is the moment the system becomes trapped inside the story it created.

Narrative is not storytelling.
Narrative is insulation.
Insulation disguised as narrative.

It is the moment the system continues believing what it used to be — even when the environment no longer allows it.

Afghanistan showed this.
Corporate governance reenacts it.
Proxy logic guarantees it.
Unintended consequences expose it.

Narrative is the architecture that keeps blindness alive after collapse becomes visible.

Chapter Three — Recurrence

Why Systems Repeat the Same Failures Even After Collapse
Afghanistan → CIA → Corporate Governance

Recurrence is not repetition.
Recurrence is the moment a system reenacts the same failure.
Because the architecture that produced the failure was never dismantled.

Afghanistan is not the CIA's first collapse.
It is one collapse in a sequence of collapses that all follow the same pattern.
identity fracture
distortion
anesthesia
acceleration
return pressure
immunity
collapse
coherence
narrative

And then — recurrence.

Recurrence is the moment the system rebuilds the same architecture that produced the collapse.
Because the architecture is part of its identity.

After Afghanistan, the CIA did not abandon proxy warfare.
It refined it.
It expanded it.
It re-justified it.
It re-narrated it.
It re-deployed it.

The institution did not say:
"Proxy warfare produces blowback."

It said:
"We need better proxies."

The institution did not say:
"We misread incentives."

It said:
"We need better intelligence."

The institution did not say:
"We empowered actors we could not control."

It said:
"We need stronger oversight."

The institution did not revise identity.
It revised technique.

This is recurrence.
The system repeats the same failure.
Because it preserves the identity that produced the failure.

The CIA reenacted the same architecture in.
Iraq
Syria
Libya
Yemen
Somalia
and multiple covert theaters that remain classified

Each operation followed the same physics.
proxies drift
incentives diverge
unintended consequences emerge
blowback returns

narrative protects identity
recurrence begins

Recurrence is not a mistake.
Recurrence is identity persistence.
Persistence disguised as inevitability.

The same physics apply to corporations.

Corporate governance reenacts the same failures with the same precision:

- vendor dependency → collapse → "we need better vendors"
- KPI distortion → collapse → "we need better dashboards"
- consultant drift → collapse → "we need better frameworks"
- offshore fragility → collapse → "we need better teams"
- strategy misalignment → collapse → "we need better data"

The enterprise does not revise identity.
It revises technique.
Technique replaces identity revision.

It does not say:
"Our architecture creates drift."

It says:
"We need better alignment."

It does not say:
"Our proxies become independent systems."

It says:
"We need stronger contracts."

It does not say:
"Our KPIs distort reality."

It says:
"We need more metrics."

Recurrence is not incompetence.
Recurrence is identity preservation.
Preservation disguised as competence.

It emerges when:

- collapse has occurred
- narrative has stabilized identity
- coherence has insulated the institution
- and the architecture remains intact

Recurrence is the third architecture of persistence.
The mechanism that ensures blindness survives collapse.

It is the moment the system rebuilds the same conditions that produced the previous collapse, because those conditions are part of its identity.

Afghanistan showed this.
Corporate governance reenacts it.
Proxy logic guarantees it.
Unintended consequences expose it.

Recurrence is not the collapse of the system.
Recurrence is the collapse of the system's ability to learn.
Learning becomes impossible.

It is the moment the institution becomes trapped in a loop of its own making — a loop where identity produces architecture, architecture produces blindness, blindness produces collapse, collapse produces narrative, narrative preserves identity, and identity produces recurrence.

Recurrence is not repetition.
Recurrence is inevitability.

It is the moment the system continues being what it used to be.
Even when the environment has already proven that identity cannot survive.

Recurrence completes persistence.
Identity remains intact.
Blindness survives collapse.
But recurrence becomes unsustainable.
Identity becomes incompatible with survival.

Section III begins when the system can no longer remain what it insists on being.

SECTION III
Prescriptive Architecture

Chapter One — Recognition

The Moment the Enterprise Finally Sees the Architecture That Has Been Running It

Recognition is not awareness.
Recognition is confrontation.

It is the moment an enterprise finally understands the architecture producing its outcomes.
The architecture it believes it operates on is not the architecture that is actually running it.

Every corporation reaches this moment eventually.
Not because leaders become wiser.
Because reality becomes unavoidable.

Recognition emerges when the enterprise can no longer rationalize.
Rationalize the contradictions it has been numbing for years.

It is the first prescriptive architecture.
The moment the system becomes visible to itself.

Case Study: The Company That Thought It Was Data-Driven

A global consumer-tech company built its identity around a single phrase.
"We are data-driven."

It appeared everywhere:

- investor calls
- strategy decks
- leadership offsites
- culture statements

- onboarding materials

The dashboards were beautiful.
The KPIs were precise.
The telemetry was real-time.

But the environment was not cooperating.
Not cooperating at all.

Customer churn rose.
Support tickets spiked.
Retention collapsed.
Competitors gained ground.

The dashboards said everything was fine.
The customers said everything was broken.
Broken in ways the dashboards could not see.

The contradiction grew until it became impossible to ignore.

A senior product leader finally said the sentence that detonated the narrative:
*"We are not data-driven.
We are dashboard-driven."*

The room went silent.

Because everyone knew it was true.

The dashboards were built on biased sampling.
The KPIs were built on misaligned incentives.
The telemetry was built on vanity metrics.
The narrative was built on internal mythology.

The enterprise wasn't data-driven.
It was **identity-driven**.
Driven by identity, not truth.

Recognition arrived the moment the enterprise confronted the truth.
"The architecture we believe we operate on is not the architecture that is actually running us."

This is recognition.

Not insight.
Not awareness.
Not learning.

Recognition is the collapse of the distance between identity and reality.

Hubris — The Human Substrate of Blindness

Hubris is not arrogance.
Hubris is not ego.
Hubris is not personality.

Hubris is **the organizational belief that it is exempt from consequence**.
Exempt from consequence entirely.

Hubris is the belief that:

- drift is temporary
- distortion is manageable
- dependency is strategic
- blowback is unlikely
- consequences are optional
- case studies apply to others
- lessons learned are theater
- "our organization is different"

Hubris is not a trait.
Hubris is an identity.

Recognition fails when hubris protects identity from truth.
Truth becomes inaccessible.

Hubris is the reason the enterprise cannot see the architecture — because seeing it would require revising identity.

Hubris is the truth the system cannot be told.

The Corporate Physics of Recognition

Recognition emerges when the enterprise can no longer protect the narrative that once defined it.

It is triggered by contradictions that become too large to anesthetize:

- KPIs contradict customer reality
- dashboards contradict market signals
- vendor dependency contradicts autonomy
- consultant drift contradicts strategy
- offshore fragility contradicts resilience
- narrative contradicts truth

Recognition is not leadership.
Recognition is consequence.

It is the moment the enterprise realizes:
*"We are not who we say we are.
We are who our architecture forces us to be."*

Recognition is the collapse of narrative insulation.

It is the moment the enterprise stops saying:
"We are different."

and begins admitting:
"We are predictable."

Recognition is not the end of blindness.
Recognition is the end of denial.

The Drift That Makes Recognition Inevitable

Every enterprise builds drift channels:

- KPIs that reward the wrong behavior
- dashboards that hide the wrong signals
- vendors that become operational backbones
- consultants that become strategists
- offshore teams that become the enterprise
- innovation labs that become theater

These channels create distance between:

- identity and operation
- narrative and truth
- leadership and consequence

Recognition is the moment that distance collapses.

It is the moment the enterprise sees:
"The architecture we built to protect ourselves is the architecture that is destroying us."

Recognition is not optional.
Recognition is structural.

It arrives when the enterprise can no longer pretend that:

- KPIs reflect reality
- dashboards reflect truth
- vendors reflect alignment
- consultants reflect capability
- offshore teams reflect resilience
- innovation labs reflect innovation

These channels create distance between:

- identity and operation
- narrative and truth
- leadership and consequence

Recognition is the moment that distance collapses.

It is the moment the enterprise sees:
"The architecture we built to protect ourselves is the architecture that is destroying us."

Recognition is not optional.
Recognition is structural.

It arrives when the enterprise can no longer pretend that:

- KPIs reflect reality
- dashboards reflect truth
- vendors reflect alignment
- consultants reflect capability
- offshore teams reflect resilience
- innovation labs reflect innovation

Recognition is the moment the enterprise confronts the future it has already created.

The Prescriptive Truth of Recognition

Recognition is not the collapse of the enterprise.
Recognition is the collapse of the enterprise's ability to lie to itself.

It is the moment the system becomes visible to itself.

Recognition is the first prescriptive architecture because nothing can be rebuilt until the enterprise admits:
"Our identity is incompatible with our environment."

Recognition is not leadership.
Recognition is consequence.

Recognition is not clarity.
Recognition is confrontation.

Recognition is not improvement.
Recognition is the beginning of transformation.

Recognition is the moment the enterprise stops reenacting the architecture that produced drift — and begins acknowledging the architecture that must be replaced.

Recognition is the first step toward survival.

Chapter Two — Revision

The Enterprise That Survives Is the Enterprise That Changes Its Identity

Revision is not adjustment.
Revision is identity reconstruction.

It is the moment the enterprise abandons the definition that produced its unintended consequences.
Not because it wants to.
Because the environment has made the old identity impossible to sustain.

Every corporation carries a narrative about itself.
"We are innovative."
"We are resilient."
"We are customer-centric."
"We are data-driven."
"We are different."

These narratives are not descriptions.
They are **identity armor**.
Armor that allows enterprises to avoid confronting the architecture that is actually running them.

Revision is the moment that armor breaks.

Case Study: The Vendor That Became the Enterprise

A Fortune 50 logistics company defined itself as "vertically integrated."
Vertically integrated as identity.

It repeated the phrase everywhere:

- investor calls
- annual reports

- strategy decks
- leadership offsites

The identity was clear.
"We control our own destiny."

But the architecture told a different story.

Over a decade, the company outsourced.
warehouse management
routing optimization
fleet maintenance
customer-service operations
last-mile delivery

Each outsourcing decision was justified as "efficiency."
Each vendor relationship was framed as "strategic."
Each dependency was treated as "temporary."

Until one vendor — a routing-optimization provider — quietly became the operational backbone of the entire enterprise.

The vendor controlled.
62% of routing decisions
78% of delivery-time predictions
91% of fleet-utilization metrics

The enterprise's identity said.
"We are vertically integrated."

The architecture said.
"We are a front-end interface for a vendor."

The fracture became undeniable.
The vendor experienced a three-day outage.

The enterprise collapsed.

Not metaphorically. Operationally.

- Deliveries halted.
- Customers churned.
- SLAs broke.
- Revenue evaporated.
- The stock dropped double digits.

The board finally confronted the truth.
"We do not control the proxy.
The proxy controls us."

This is the moment of revision.

Not when the outage happened.
Not when the vendor drifted.
Not when the architecture shifted.

Revision arrived when the enterprise finally admitted.
"Our identity is incompatible with our environment."

Hubris — The Enemy of Revision

Hubris is not arrogance.
Hubris is not ego.
Hubris is not personality.

Hubris is **the organizational belief that it is exempt from consequence.**

Hubris is the belief that:

- "We are vertically integrated."
- "We are data driven."
- "We are resilient."
- "We are different."

even when the architecture proves otherwise.

Hubris is the refusal of permission — permission to revise identity, permission to confront architecture, permission to absorb truth.

Revision fails when hubris protects narrative from consequence.
Consequence becomes invisible.

Hubris is the reason enterprises reenact the same architecture and expect different outcomes.

Hubris is the truth the system cannot be told — because telling it would require dismantling the identity that leaders depend on for legitimacy.

The Corporate Physics of Revision

Revision is not about changing the narrative.
Revision is about changing the **definition**.

The enterprise must abandon the identity that produced drift, distortion, and dependency — because that identity cannot survive the conditions the enterprise actually operates in.

Revision requires confronting truths that feel destabilizing.
"We are not data-driven."
"We are not vertically integrated."
"We are not customer-centric."
"We are not resilient."
"We are not different."

These sentences are not admissions.
They are **architectural corrections.**

Revision is the moment the enterprise stops asking:
"How do we fix the architecture?"

and begins asking:
"Who do we need to become so this architecture never forms again?"

Revision is identity reconstruction.

It is the moment the enterprise replaces:

- narrative identity → with operational identity
- aspirational identity → with environmental identity
- historical identity → with survival identity

Revision is not improvement.
Revision is transformation.

The Drift That Makes Revision Necessary

Enterprises resist revision because identity feels stable.

But identity is often the source of drift.

Drift emerges when:

- KPIs reward the wrong behavior
- dashboards hide the wrong signals
- vendors become operational backbones
- consultants become strategists
- offshore teams become the enterprise
- innovation labs become theater

These drift channels form because the enterprise protects identity instead of revising it.

The logistics company protected "vertical integration" long after it had become a myth.

Your enterprise protects its own myths too.

Every enterprise does.

Revision is the moment the enterprise stops protecting the identity that produced drift — and begins dismantling the architecture that reenacts it.

The Prescriptive Truth of Revision

Revision is not the collapse of identity.
Revision is the collapse of identity **illusion**.

It is the moment the enterprise becomes capable of survival because it becomes capable of truth.

Revision requires:

- abandoning narratives
- confronting architecture
- redefining identity
- rebuilding incentives
- reconnecting operation to reality

Revision is the moment the enterprise says:
"We will no longer define ourselves by what we want to be. We will define ourselves by what the environment requires us to be."

Revision is not optional.
Revision is structural.

It is the second prescriptive architecture — the moment the enterprise becomes capable of becoming something new.

Chapter Three — Rearchitecture

The Enterprise Must Replace the Channels That Produced Blindness

Rearchitecture is not optimization.
Rearchitecture is structural replacement.

It is the moment the enterprise stops trying to fix the channels that produced drift, distortion, and dependency.
And begins dismantling them..

Every corporation believes it can repair its architecture.
None can.

Because the architecture is not broken.
It is doing exactly what it was designed to do.

Rearchitecture is the moment the enterprise finally admits.
"The system is not malfunctioning.
The system is functioning exactly as built — and that is the problem."

Case Study: The Consultant That Became the Company

A major financial institution outsourced its strategy to a consulting firm.
For eight consecutive years.

The consultants were originally hired to.
"accelerate transformation"
"bring external perspective"
"increase strategic clarity"

But over time, the consultants became.
the authors of every strategy deck
the owners of every roadmap
the arbiters of every KPI

the interpreters of every dashboard
the designers of every initiative

The enterprise's identity said.
"We lead. Consultants advise."

The architecture said.
"Consultants lead. We reenact."

The drift was subtle at first.

Executives began deferring decisions.
Directors began waiting for "the deck."
Managers began asking, "What did the consultants say?"
Teams began optimizing for consultant-defined KPIs.

The consultants became the de facto leadership.
The enterprise became the implementation arm.
Implementation without leadership.

The fracture became undeniable.
A regulatory change required rapid strategic adaptation.

The consultants could not respond.
They did not understand the operational reality.
They did not understand the customer.
They did not understand the constraints.

The enterprise froze.

Not because it lacked intelligence.
Because it lacked architecture.

The board finally confronted the truth.
"We outsourced strategy.
We outsourced identity.
We outsourced ourselves."

Rearchitecture became unavoidable.

Hubris — The Enemy of Rearchitecture

Hubris is not arrogance.
Hubris is not ego.
Hubris is not personality.

Hubris is **the organizational belief that it is exempt from consequence.**

Hubris is the belief that:

- vendor dependency is strategic
- consultant capture is temporary
- offshore fragility is manageable
- KPI distortion is fixable
- dashboard blindness is a data problem
- innovation-lab theater is innovation

Hubris is the belief that drift channels can be controlled.
Even when the architecture proves otherwise.

Hubris is the refusal of permission:
permission to dismantle proxies,
permission to rebuild capability,
permission to confront dependency,
permission to absorb consequence.

Rearchitecture fails when hubris protects drift channels from dismantling.

Hubris is the reason enterprises try to keep the architecture and change the outcomes.

They cannot.

Hubris is the truth the system cannot be told — because telling it would require dismantling the identity leaders depend on for legitimacy.

The Corporate Physics of Rearchitecture

Rearchitecture is not about improving the channels.
It is about replacing them.

Blindness emerges from drift channels.
vendor dependency
consultant capture
offshore fragility
KPI distortion
dashboard blindness
innovation-lab theater

These channels cannot be repaired because they are not accidental.
They are structural.

Vendor dependency is not a failure.
It is the architecture.

Consultant capture is not a mistake.
It is the architecture.

Offshore fragility is not an anomaly.
It is the architecture.

KPI distortion is not misalignment.
It is the architecture.

Dashboard blindness is not a data problem.
It is the architecture.

Innovation-lab theater is not a culture problem.
It is the architecture.

Rearchitecture is the moment the enterprise stops trying to fix these channels.
And begins replacing them with channels that produce alignment.

The Drift That Makes Rearchitecture Necessary

Drift channels form because the enterprise protects identity instead of revising it.

When identity fractures, the enterprise builds proxies:

- vendors to absorb operational load
- consultants to absorb strategic load
- offshore teams to absorb cost pressure
- dashboards to absorb narrative pressure
- KPIs to absorb leadership pressure
- innovation labs to absorb cultural pressure

Each proxy becomes a drift channel.
Each drift channel becomes an unintended consequence.
Each unintended consequence becomes a future the enterprise cannot survive.

Rearchitecture is the moment the enterprise confronts the truth:
"We cannot fix drift.
We must eliminate the channels that produce drift."

The Prescriptive Truth of Rearchitecture

Rearchitecture is not the collapse of the old system.
Rearchitecture is the collapse of the old system's permission to exist.

It requires:

- eliminating consultant capture
- dismantling vendor dependency
- rebuilding internal capability
- reconnecting incentives to operational truth
- replacing dashboards with real feedback
- replacing KPIs with customer reality

- replacing innovation labs with operational innovation

Rearchitecture is the moment the enterprise stops reenacting the architecture that produced collapse — and begins constructing the architecture that prevents it.

Rearchitecture is not optional.
Rearchitecture is structural.

It is the third prescriptive architecture — the moment the enterprise becomes capable of replacing the system that created its unintended consequences.

Chapter Four — Reintegration

The Enterprise Must Reconnect Identity, Incentives, Architecture, and Reality

Reintegration is not alignment.
Reintegration is coherence.

Blindness fractures a corporation into pieces.
identity
incentives
architecture
operation
consequence
narrative

Each becomes its own orbit.
Each becomes its own truth.
Each becomes its own justification.

Reintegration is the moment those orbits collapse.
Collapse back into a single system.

It is the moment the enterprise stops operating as a collection of disconnected parts.
And begins functioning as an organism again.

Case Study: The KPI That Broke the Company

A SaaS company optimized for a single metric.
monthly active users.

The KPI became the identity.
The identity became the architecture.
The architecture became the operation.

Teams optimized for activity, not value.
Product decisions optimized for clicks, not outcomes.

Marketing optimized for acquisition, not retention.
Support optimized for ticket closure, not resolution.

The enterprise grew users but lost customers.

The fracture was total.
identity drift
incentive distortion
architectural misalignment
operational contradiction
narrative inflation

The company believed it was "growing."
The environment showed it was collapsing.
Collapsing beneath its own architecture.

Reintegration began when leadership confronted the truth.
"We are not a SaaS company with a retention problem.
We are a retention problem reenacting a SaaS company."

Reintegration required reconnecting.
identity → to customer reality
incentives → to retention
architecture → to resilience
operation → to consequence
narrative → to truth

Reintegration is not alignment.
Reintegration is the collapse of illusion.

Hubris — The Enemy of Reintegration

Hubris is the belief that incentives can drift without consequence.

Hubris is the belief that.
KPIs define reality
dashboards define truth

proxies define capability
narratives define identity

Hubris protects incentives from alignment.
Hubris protects architecture from consequence.
Hubris protects narrative from reality.

Reintegration fails when hubris insists.
"The parts are fine.
The system is fine.
The future is fine."

Reintegration is the moment the enterprise stops protecting the parts.
And begins reconstructing the system.

The Corporate Physics of Reintegration

Reintegration requires collapsing the distance between.
identity and operation
incentives and consequence
architecture and environment
narrative and truth

This collapse is violent.

Because reintegration requires confronting the contradictions that leaders have been protecting for years.

Reintegration is the moment the enterprise admits.
"Our incentives are producing the outcomes we claim to be trying to avoid."

Reintegration is the moment the enterprise stops optimizing for metrics.
And begins optimizing for reality.

Reintegration is not optional.
Reintegration is structural.

It is the fourth prescriptive architecture — the moment the enterprise becomes capable of coherence.

Chapter Five — Continuity

The Enterprise That Survives Is the Enterprise That Maintains Alignment Over Time

Continuity is not stability.
Continuity is vigilance.

It is the moment the enterprise builds mechanisms that prevent future blindness.
Not by predicting the future.
But by remaining aligned with reality regardless of the future.

Continuity is the architecture of survival.

Case Study: The Innovation Lab That Became a Mirage

A global tech company built an "innovation lab" to stay ahead of disruption.
A lab built as identity armor.

The lab produced prototypes.
The prototypes produced press.
The press produced narrative.

But none of the prototypes reached customers.
Not one.

The lab became a theater.
A place where innovation was performed, not produced.

The enterprise believed it was "innovating."
The environment showed it was stagnating.

Continuity required dismantling the lab.
And rebuilding innovation inside the operational core.
Where incentives, architecture, and reality were aligned.

Continuity is not the preservation of innovation.
Continuity is the preservation of truth.

Hubris — The Enemy of Continuity

Hubris is the belief that vigilance is optional.

Hubris is the belief that.
feedback can be anesthetized
KPIs can be gamed
dashboards can be curated
incentives can drift
governance can be insulated
narrative can detach from truth

Hubris protects the future from feedback.

Continuity fails when hubris insists.
"We will always be what we once were."

Continuity is the moment the enterprise abandons nostalgia.
And begins constructing mechanisms that prevent drift.

The Corporate Physics of Continuity

Continuity requires.
feedback channels that cannot be anesthetized
KPIs that cannot be distorted
dashboards that cannot be gamed
incentives that cannot drift
governance that cannot be insulated
narrative that cannot detach from truth

Continuity is not the end of drift.
Continuity is the prevention of drift.

Continuity is the moment the enterprise becomes capable of surviving the future it creates.
Surviving the future instead of reenacting the past.

Continuity is not optional.
Continuity is structural.

It is the fifth prescriptive architecture.
The moment the enterprise becomes capable of sustaining coherence over time.

Continuity stabilizes the enterprise.
Stability is not emergence.
Section III reconstructs the system.
Reconstruction is preparation.
Emergence begins where continuity ends.
When the system becomes capable of becoming something the old architecture could not sustain

Transition — *The Moment the System Becomes Capable of Becoming Something New*

The prescriptive arc is not the end of blindness.
It is the end of the system's ability to reenact blindness.

Recognition collapses denial.
Revision collapses identity illusion.
Rearchitecture collapses drift channels.
Reintegration collapses fragmentation.
Continuity collapses future blindness.

But the prescriptive arc does not produce a new system.
It produces the conditions for one.

It produces the moment when the enterprise becomes structurally incapable of remaining what it was.
Incapable of reenacting the identity that produced collapse.
Incapable of returning to the architecture that made blindness inevitable.

This is the moment the system stops reenacting the physics of collapse.
This is the moment the system begins constructing the physics that prevent collapse.

But construction is not emergence.
Construction is preparation.

Preparation is the work of rebuilding coherence.
Preparation is the work of restoring identity integrity.
Preparation is the work of eliminating reenactment channels.
Preparation is the work of removing the system's ability to collapse in familiar ways.

Preparation is the work of becoming capable of becoming something new.

Emergence is not the construction of a new system.
Emergence is the moment the system becomes capable of surviving the future it creates.
Surviving the future instead of collapsing under it.

Emergence is the moment the system becomes capable of becoming something new.

SECTION IV
Emergence Architecture

Terminal Chapter — Emergence

The System That Survives Its Own Collapse

Emergence is not recovery.
Emergence is not resilience.
Emergence is not adaptation.

Emergence is **continuity after collapse**.
The moment the system becomes capable of surviving the futures it creates.

Collapse is not the end of the system.
Collapse is the end of the system's ability to lie to itself.

Emergence is what happens next.

The System That Survives Is Not the System That Collapsed

The system that collapses is defined by.
identity fracture
distortion
anesthesia
acceleration
return pressure
immunity

The system that emerges is defined by.
recognition
revision
rearchitecture
reintegration
continuity

Emergence is not the continuation of the old system.
Emergence is the arrival of a system that could not exist under the old architecture.

The system that collapses protects identity.
The system that emerges protects truth.

The system that collapses numbs contradiction.
The system that emerges absorbs contradiction.

The system that collapses accelerates drift.
The system that emerges eliminates drift channels.

The system that collapses reenacts proxies.
The system that emerges dismantles proxies.

The system that collapses believes it is exempt from consequence.
The system that emerges understands consequence as architecture.

Emergence is not improvement.
Emergence is replacement.

Hubris — The Human Layer That Must Be Dismantled for Emergence to Occur

Hubris is the belief that the system is exempt from consequence.

Hubris is the belief that:

- "We are different."
- "We are resilient."
- "We are data driven."
- "We are vertically integrated."
- "We can control this."

Hubris is the identity that collapses the system.

Emergence is the identity that replaces it.

Emergence requires dismantling hubris.
Not by punishing it.
Not by shaming it.
But by making it structurally impossible.

Emergence is the moment the system becomes incapable of reenacting the identity that produced collapse.

Emergence Is the Architecture of Survival

Emergence is not a return to stability.
Emergence is the arrival of a system that can survive instability.

Emergence requires.
identity defined by environment
incentives defined by consequence
architecture defined by reality
operation defined by truth
governance defined by alignment
narrative defined by accuracy

Emergence is the moment the system becomes capable of absorbing the futures it creates.
Instead of being destroyed by them.

Emergence is not optional.
Emergence is structural.

It is the final movement of the book.
The moment the system becomes capable of surviving itself.

Emergence Is the End of Blindness

Blindness is not the absence of information.
Blindness is the refusal of information.

Emergence is the moment refusal becomes impossible.

Emergence is the moment the system becomes capable of.
seeing itself
revising itself
replacing itself
reintegrating itself
sustaining itself

Emergence is the moment the system becomes capable of truth.

Not because it wants to.
Because it must.

Emergence is the system that survives its own collapse.

APPENDIX

APPENDIX A — The Consultants That Became the Company (McKinsey & Eskom)

Every collapsing system produces a moment when leadership no longer leads. Decisions still occur, but they no longer originate inside the institution. They originate inside the proxy the institution hired to think for it. The collapse is not financial. It is architectural. The enterprise loses the ability to generate its own future.

Eskom, South Africa's national power utility, reached this moment long before the first blackout. McKinsey had become the de facto strategist. Internal capability eroded. Executives deferred decisions. Directors waited for decks. Managers asked what the consultants thought. The utility became an implementation arm for a strategy it did not create.

Public reporting captured the fracture clearly: "McKinsey effectively ran Eskom's strategy."

The consultants did not drift because they were malicious. They drifted because their incentives were external. Their loyalty was contractual. Their horizon was quarterly. Their architecture was extraction. Eskom believed it was buying clarity. It was buying dependency.

The collapse arrived when the environment demanded decisions the consultants could not make. The grid destabilized. Maintenance backlogs grew. Operational risk multiplied. The consultants froze because they did not understand the operational substrate. Eskom froze because it no longer remembered how to think.

This was not incompetence. It was not arrogance. It was not denial.

It was the architecture of a system that could not tell the truth about itself without dismantling the proxy it depended on for survival.

Consultant capture is not a failure. Consultant capture is identity fracture made operational.

Eskom did not collapse because consultants drifted. Eskom collapsed because it outsourced the ability to prevent drift.

The consultants were not the frog. The consultants were the water.

APPENDIX B — The Scheduled Collapse (Hunter Boot)

The story of Hunter Boot is often told as a sequence of unfortunate events. Demand softened in 2019. Brexit introduced friction. Covid disrupted supply chains. Inflation eroded margins. These are the explanations that appear in articles and postmortems. They are tidy. They are familiar. They are wrong. They describe the weather and ignore the physics. The collapse of Hunter was not caused by external shocks. It was caused by the capital structure that made those shocks unabsorbable. The outcome was written the day Searchlight acquired the company.

When a private equity firm takes control of an operator, the business is not simply purchased. It is reconfigured. The operating company becomes the debt vehicle. The brand becomes the collateral. The resilience disappears. The tolerance for volatility collapses. The survival of the company becomes conditional on perfect seasons and uninterrupted demand. From that moment forward, collapse is not a possibility. It is a scheduled event. The only unknown is timing.

Observers narrate the visible turbulence and miss the structural failure that made turbulence fatal. They say leverage was fine while demand held. They say the softening in 2019 was the turning point. They say Brexit and Covid accelerated the decline. These explanations are comfortable because they preserve the illusion that the business was healthy until external forces intervened. But the business was not healthy. It was already terminal. The external forces did not cause the collapse. They revealed it.

The moment Searchlight rewrote the capital structure, Hunter lost the ability to absorb normal volatility. Retail demand is never stable. Seasons fluctuate. Weather shifts. Fashion cycles move. Costs rise. These variations are survivable for a business with resilience. They are fatal for a business whose operating company has been converted into a leveraged extraction vehicle. The venom enters the bloodstream at acquisition. The body continues to walk for a while. The moment of collapse is determined not by the severity of external shocks but by the speed at which the venom reaches the heart.

This is why suppliers continued to ship inventory long after the danger was visible. They knew private equity ownership was dangerous. They knew the cultural pattern. They knew the reputations of the firms involved. They knew the stories. Yet they continued to extend credit. They continued to forecast next year's revenue. They continued to behave as if the system were stable. This was not optimism. It was not incompetence. It was not denial. It was the structural impossibility of acting on the truth inside a system that would destroy itself the moment it acknowledged reality.

Suppliers cannot cut credit without triggering their own collapse. They cannot reduce projections without triggering a death spiral inside their own organization. They cannot warn shareholders without damaging their own valuation. They cannot see the timing of the collapse because the timing is hidden inside lender negotiations and covenant breaches they are never allowed to see. They know the story. They do not know the clock. And timing is everything.

The blindness is not emotional. It is architectural. The system forces every participant to behave as if the water is warm even when the water is already boiling. The collapse arrives suddenly. The wipeout is total. The supplier pays the price because the supplier is structurally unsecured, structurally uninformed, and structurally trapped.

The author who narrates Hunter's demise as a consequence of Brexit, Covid, and inflation is describing symptoms. The cause was embedded in the capital stack years earlier.

This is the blindness protocol. The collapse is known. The narrative remains optimistic. The outcome is scheduled. The participants continue to behave as if the water is perfect.

The frog is not blind. The frog is trapped.

APPENDIX C — The Financialization of Scarcity (NBA)

The NBA's decision to allow private equity funds to purchase minority stakes in franchises is often described as modernization. It is framed as liquidity, diversification, estate planning, and professionalization. These are the narratives used to make the change appear neutral. But the structural reality is different. The moment private equity enters a scarcity asset class, the asset class is no longer defined by its cultural function. It becomes a financial instrument. The physics of the system change. The incentives change. The valuation dynamics change. The truth becomes something the system cannot acknowledge without undermining its own legitimacy.

NBA franchises are scarcity assets. Only thirty exist. None are created. None are destroyed. Demand is global. Supply is fixed. Scarcity alone creates valuation pressure. But scarcity combined with institutional capital creates something else. It creates financialization. Private equity does not need control to extract value. It needs exposure. The moment a private equity fund is allowed to buy a minority stake, the franchise becomes part of a portfolio. The portfolio becomes part of a fund. The fund becomes part of a market. The market becomes part of a valuation curve. The valuation curve becomes the extraction surface.

This is not operational extraction. Private equity cannot lever the team. It cannot force management changes. It cannot dictate strategy. It cannot sweep cash. It cannot restructure the operator. The league prohibits all of that. But the league cannot prohibit valuation appreciation. It cannot prohibit liquidity. It cannot prohibit competitive bidding. It cannot prohibit secondary markets. It cannot prohibit exit velocity. Private equity extracts at the fund level, not the team level. That is the mechanism. That is the architecture.

The moment private equity enters, valuation rises. It rises because institutional capital increases liquidity. It rises because buyer competition increases. It rises because exit pathways multiply. It rises because scarcity becomes financialized. The rise in valuation is not caused by operational improvement. It is caused by the presence of private equity itself. The entrance is the pump. The exit is the dump. The extraction is the delta between the valuation at entry and the valuation at exit. Nothing needs to happen inside the franchise. The extraction occurs entirely outside the operator.

The league cannot say this. It cannot admit that it has allowed a mechanism that inflates valuations through financial positioning rather than performance. It cannot admit that minority stakes create a market dynamic that rewards appreciation rather than contribution. It cannot admit that private equity can buy, hold briefly, and exit with a gain without ever touching operations. It cannot admit that scarcity assets become financial instruments the moment institutional capital enters. The league must maintain the narrative that this is modernization. The truth would destabilize the legitimacy of the asset class.

This is the blindness protocol. The system cannot tell the truth about what it has allowed because telling the truth would expose the structural corruption of the ownership market. The participants cannot acknowledge the mechanism because acknowledging it would undermine the narrative that franchises are cultural institutions rather than financial products. The owners cannot acknowledge it because they benefit from the inflation. The league cannot acknowledge it because it benefits from the stability. Private equity will never acknowledge it because the extraction depends on the blindness.

The physics are simple. Scarcity assets inflate when institutional capital enters. Private equity extracts by riding the inflation curve it helps create. The extraction is legal. It is institutional. It is sanitized. It is invisible to the narrative layer. It is obvious at the architectural layer. It is the same blindness that appears in leveraged retail, in supplier ecosystems, in collapsing operators, and in every system where incentives distort truth. The domain changes. The physics do not.

This appendix exists because the mechanism is universal. The blindness is universal. The architecture is universal. The NBA is not an exception. It is another example of a system that cannot tell the truth about itself without triggering consequences it cannot absorb.

www.ingramcontent.com/pod-product-compliance
Lightning Source LLC
LaVergne TN
LVHW010736061126
851857LV00014B/1510

* 9 7 9 8 9 9 7 1 0 1 3 3 6 *